HANDS-ON HISTORY

PROJECTS ABOUT

American Indians of the Southwest

Marian Broida

BENCHMARK BOOKS

MARSHALL CAVENDISH
NEW YORK

Acknowledgments

Thanks to the following individuals and groups for their assistance: Suzan Craig, education specialist, Anasazi Heritage Center; Rita Edaakie, Zuni tradition bearer, A:shiwi A:wan Museum and Heritage Center; Marvin Lalo, Hopi language program coordinator, Hopi Cultural Preservation Office; Robert Johnson, Navajo cultural specialist, and Norman Bahe, museum education curator, Navajo Nation Museum.

For their help in testing activities: Lynne Ravatt, teacher at View Ridge Elementary, and the fifth-grade classes of 2001–2002; View Ridge Boys' and Girls' Club; Shaina Andres, Veronica Bardue, Zoe Baxter, Nicole Klionsky, and Beatrice Misher.

The quote on page 6 is abbreviated from "American Indian Philosophy and Its Relation to the Modern World" by Alfonso Ortiz, in *Indian Voices: The First Convocation of American Indian Scholars*. San Francisco: The Indian Historian Press, 1970.

Benchmark Books
Marshall Cavendish
99 White Plains Road
Tarrytown, NY 10591-9001
www.marshallcavendish.com

Library of Congress Cataloging-in-Publication Data

Broida, Marian.
  Projects about the Indians of the American Southwest / by Marian
Broida.
     v. cm. -- (Hands-on history)
Includes bibliographical references and index.
Contents: Introduction -- Traditional homes of the Southwest Indians --
Ancient Pueblo people -- The Navajo -- The Hopi and Zuni.
ISBN 0-7614-1602-1
1. Indians of North America--Southwest, New--Juvenile literature. 2.
Indian craft--Juvenile literature. [1. Indians of North
America--Southwest, New. 2. Indian craft.] I. Title. II. Series.

E78.S7B76 2004
979.004'97--dc21
                                    2002155874

Illustrations and map by Rodica Prato

Printed in China

1 3 5 6 4 2

Contents

ༀ

The east and west "Mitten" buttes of Monument
Valley, located within the Navajo reservation on the
Utah/Arizona border.

1

Introduction

The American Southwest—Arizona, New Mexico, and parts of Texas, Colorado, Utah, and Nevada—has been home to American Indians for thousands of years. If you were to take a few steps in the dry, sandy soil, you would be walking in the footprints of people who lived long before history began.

This book will help you to understand the ways of these people. You will do the activities your own way, using ideas or techniques inspired by American Indians. You will visit ancient **Pueblo** people who lived nine hundred years ago. You will meet Zuni, Hopi, and Navajo Indians living at different times over the past two hundred years.

You will weave, build a model garden, paint rocks, and make a buzz toy. To many Southwest Indians, a bowl is more than just a bowl. It carries the stories of those who made it and ate from it. The land is more than a place to walk on. It carries the spirits of their ancestors.

Today, some Southwest Indians live in **hogans**, the traditional Navajo homes of wood and mud. Others live in pueblos, villages made of stone or **adobe**. These dwellings are much like the ones their ancestors used. Still other Southwest Indians live in modern apartments and houses. Wherever they live, Southwest Indians may follow some of the "old ways," praying and celebrating as their ancestors did and learning the languages their grandparents spoke.

As the Navajo people say, *Yá-át-ééh!*—Greetings!

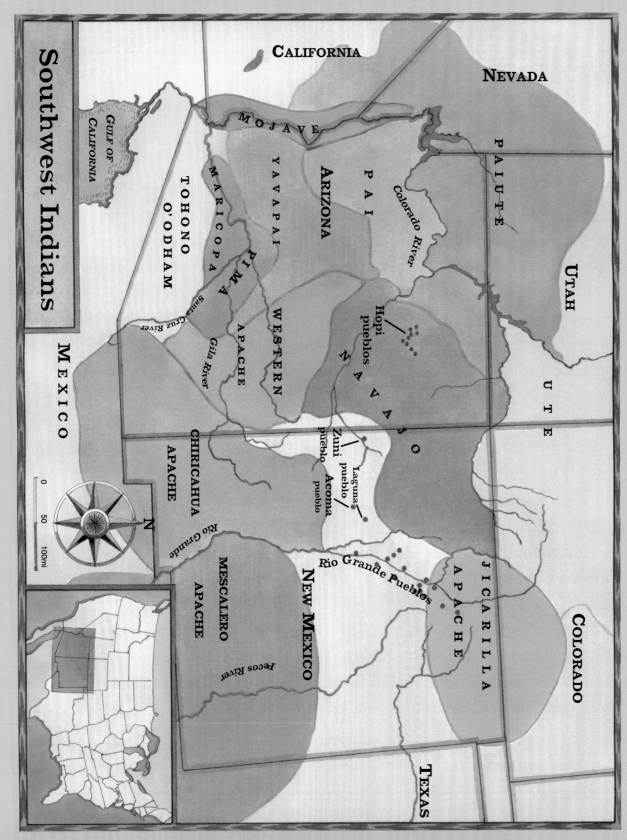

Southwest Indians

This map shows the traditional homelands of many American Indian tribes or nations in the Southwest. The red dots represent Pueblo nations. The Hopi pueblos are located within Navajo territory.

CALIFORNIA

NEVADA

UTAH

COLORADO

ARIZONA

NEW MEXICO

TEXAS

MEXICO

GULF OF CALIFORNIA

MOJAVE

PAIUTE

UTE

PAI

YAVAPAI

NAVAJO

TOHONO O'ODHAM

MARICOPA

PIMA

WESTERN APACHE

CHIRICAHUA APACHE

MESCALERO APACHE

JICARILLA APACHE

Colorado River

Santa Cruz River

Gila River

Rio Grande

Pecos River

Hopi pueblos

Zuni pueblo

Acoma pueblo

Laguna pueblo

Rio Grande Pueblos

N

0   50   100mi

Traditional Homes of the Southwest Indians

The landscape of the American Southwest includes parched deserts and snow-topped mountains. This land and the animals and plants that live there are **sacred**, or holy, to the people. As a Pueblo man once said, "The story of my people and the story of this place are one single story. We are always joined together." Here's how to pronounce the names of some Southwest Indian nations. Not all of these appear on the map.

Acoma Pueblo (AH-ko-ma PWEB-loh)

Anasazi (a-nah-SAH-zee)

Chiricahua Apache (CHEE-ree-KAH-wah a-PATCH-ee)

Hopi (HO-pee)

Jicarilla Apache (hee-ka-REE-ya a-PATCH-ee)

Laguna Pueblo (la-GOO-na PWEB-loh)

Maricopa (mar-ee-KO-pa)

Mescalero Apache (mess-kah-LAY-ro a-PATCH-ee)

Mogollon (moggy-OWN)

Mojave (mo-HAH-vee)

Navajo (NAV-a-ho)

Pai (PIE)

Paiute (PA-yoot)

Pima (PEE-ma)

Rio Grande Pueblos (REE-oh GRAND PWEB-loze)

Tohono O'odham (TOE-hoe-no OH-oh-dom)

Ute (YOOT)

Yavapai (Yah-vah-pie)

Zuni (ZOON-ee)

In many pueblos, flat-roofed homes are stacked one atop another to form apartment buildings. This ancient pueblo, called Cliff Palace, had 220 rooms and 23 kivas—special areas for religious ceremonies.

2

Ancient Pueblo People

Long before Columbus crossed the ocean, ancient Pueblo people built two great civilizations in the Southwest. Today, one of these is often called Anasazi, and the other Mogollon. These societies lasted more than a thousand years. The Anasazi in the northern region and the Mogollon in the south were the ancestors of modern Pueblo Indians.

Some people do not like the name Anasazi, because it comes from a Navajo word that means ancient enemies. They prefer Pueblo ancestors or ancient Pueblos.

Ancient Pueblo people were farmers, living in villages of stone or adobe. Some of these villages, also called pueblos, had four or five floors and hundreds of rooms. Amazingly, ancient Pueblos built these villages without the help of engines, horses, or even wheels.

Pueblo Homes

The year is A.D. 1123. You are visiting an ancient Pueblo home. A boy beckons you from the flat roof. His house is built of sandstone blocks covered with clay plaster. It is shaped like a long box.

You climb up a ladder leaning against the house and scramble onto the roof. A second ladder juts from a square hole in the rooftop. The boy climbs down into the house. You follow, a little nervous.

Inside, the only light comes from the opening by which you entered. In a corner are two large flat stones for grinding corn. Wood beams hold up the roof. As you enter, the boy's family greets you.

The Acoma pueblo in New Mexico was built in the year 1150.

1. Spread newspaper over your work surface.

2. Turn the tissue box upside down. Cut a square hole 1½ to 2 inches wide in the middle of the bottom of the tissue box.

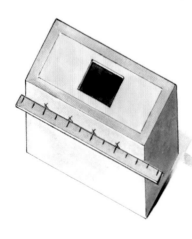

3. Using the ruler, draw an X every 2 inches along one long side of the box, about 1 inch from the bottom (where you cut the hole). You will have four or five Xs.

4. Draw Xs the same way on the other long side. Start measuring from the same end of the box, to make sure your second row of Xs is exactly opposite the first.

5. Poke the nail through each X.

11

6. Paint the box. Sprinkle the wet paint with sand or cornmeal to make it look like clay plaster or adobe.

7. After the paint dries, push a chopstick through the first hole until it sticks out the hole on the other side. If you need to, enlarge the holes with the pen. Fill all the holes this way.

8. Make two ladders. Cut the pipe cleaners into thirds. Lay two chopsticks side by side. Use four or five pipe cleaner pieces for rungs. Make sure the ladder can fit through the hole in the box. Repeat with remaining chopsticks and pipe-cleaner pieces.

9. Place one ladder in the hole. Lean the other against the outside of the box.

Rock Painting

You are traveling through Arizona during your summer vacation. You gaze at red and white paintings on a rock wall. Handprints stand out beside pictures that look like people.

"Ancient Pueblo people painted these more than a thousand years ago," says the guide.

"What were the paintings for?" you ask.

"We're not sure," says the guide. "They might have been for religious purposes. Or perhaps people made handprints the way we sign our names today."

You want to touch the pictures, but you know better. Who were the painters, you wonder. What stories could they tell us about their lives?

This rock painting was done between A.D. 500 and 1500.

You will need:

- large flat rock
- damp rag
- newspaper
- paint brushes
- jar of water
- tempura or acrylic paints, brick-red and white, or make your own paints (see page 14)

When painting your rock, imagine someone finding it a thousand years from now. What would your painting tell them?

1. Scrub the rock with a damp rag, and let it dry.

2. Spread out some newspaper, and put the rock on top.

3. Paint the rock with people, animals, or other designs. If you have a large enough rock, paint the palm of one hand and press it on the rock. Use the jar of water to clean the brushes if you use more than one color.

To make paint

The ancient Pueblos made paint from clay and other minerals. They ground them up, mixed them with something sticky—such as **yucca** juice or egg white—and added water.

You will need:

- walnut-sized piece of reddish potter's clay
- newspaper
- sandpaper
- 4 clean, dry jars with lids. Baby-food jars work well.
- stick of white chalk
- hammer
- raw eggs
- measuring spoons
- two small spoons
- bowl of water

1. Flatten the clay, and let it dry in a warm place on a piece of newspaper. This may take several days.

2. For red paint, sand the dried clay over the newspaper until you have at least one tablespoon of powder. Pour the powder into one of the jars.

3. For white paint, put the chalk inside a folded newspaper. Pound it with a hammer until it turns to powder. Do not leave any tiny chunks. Carefully pour the chalk powder into another jar.

4. Have an adult help you collect egg white this way: Have two jars handy. Hit the egg on a jar rim, firmly. Hold the egg upright and remove the top piece of shell. Pour the egg white into one jar, then pour the yolk into the other. Use the yolk for something else or throw it away.

5. Measure ¼ teaspoon of egg white into each jar of powder. Stir with a clean, dry spoon until egg white touches all the powder. (Use a different spoon for each mixture.) Take your time. If some of the powder remains dry, add another ¼ teaspoon of egg white—no more.

6. Add ½ teaspoon of water to each jar. Mix again. If one of the mixtures is too thick, add more water, ¼ teaspoon at a time, stirring each time. Be careful not to add too much water.

7. Cap the paint jars. Use the paint within a day, or it may get moldy and smell bad.

A Navajo Indian on horseback looks out over Monument Valley.

3

The Navajo

The Navajo call themselves the Diné, which means people in their own language. Their **reservation** stretches over parts of three states: New Mexico, Utah, and Arizona. Different types of homes are scattered across it: modern-style houses, trailers, and one-room hogans made of logs, the rounded roofs covered with earth.

Some Navajo people raise sheep and weave rugs, much as their grandparents did. Others make elegant jewelry of silver and **turquoise.** Many have modern jobs but still follow their traditions.

A Navajo log hogan

A woman could work about two hundred hours to make a 3-by-5-foot blanket. With all of her other chores, it might take several months to complete it.

Navajo Weaving

It is 1850. Outside, two women sit before a tall loom strung with wool yarn. "This is the proper month to teach you to weave," the older woman tells her adult daughter. "This is the month that black spiders come out. It's the same month that a Holy Person named Spider Woman taught First Woman to weave. First Woman was another Holy Person who lived before humans like us were created."

The older Woman shows her daughter where to put her hands on the loom. "When you were a baby, we rubbed your hands with spiderwebs," she says, "so that you would be a good weaver."

> ## You will need:
>
> - ruler
> - pencil or pen
> - heavy cardboard, about 8 by 12 inches
> - yarn, regular weight: 11 yards of one color, 30 yards of another color
> - strong scissors
> - large paper clip
> - chopstick or paintbrush, at least 9 inches long

Once it is finished, you can hang your weaving on the wall, use it as a mat for a piece of pottery, or stitch the sides together to make a little bag.

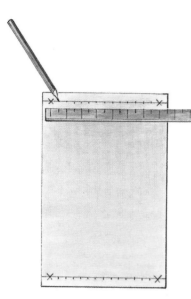

1. To make the loom, use the ruler to draw a line across each short end of the cardboard, about half an inch from the edge. Measure and mark dots every half inch along each line. Make an X over the first and last dots on each end.

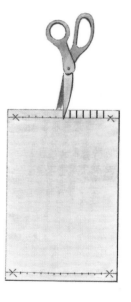

2. Cut a slit from the edge to each dot, except for the ones with the Xs.

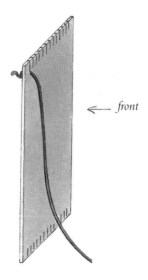

← *front*

3. Knot one end of the 11-yard-long piece of yarn. (You can leave it in a ball.) Thread it through an end slit on top of the loom, so the ruled lines are facing you and the knot is in back. Bring the yarn down the front of the cardboard, through the matching slit on the other end, around the back, through the next slit on top, down the front, and so on, until you've used all the slits. Knot the other end behind the last bottom slit. This yarn is your **warp**.

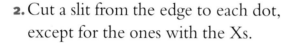

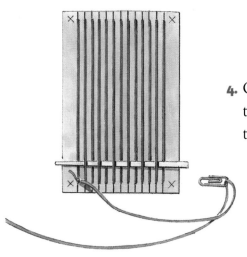

4. Cut a piece of yarn 3 to 4 feet long. Tie one end to the warp near one of the lower corners. Loosely tie the other end to your paper clip.

5. To weave, push the stick under every other thread, near the bottom of the loom. Now pull the paper clip and yarn through the tunnel you've made, just below the stick. Leave the yarn loose. Pulling it tight will make the sides of the weaving squeeze in.

6. Push the yarn down into an even line with the stick. Pull out the stick. Now push it under all the threads you skipped the first time. (It goes over the ones it went under before, and under the ones it went over.) Pull the paper clip and yarn through the new tunnel from the other direction. Push the yarn down with the stick.

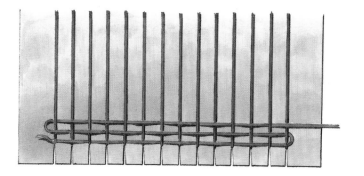

7. Untie the paper clip when about 3 inches of yarn are still unwoven. Tie a new piece of yarn, 3 to 4 feet long, onto the old one. (You can trim the ends when you finish.) Tie the new piece to the paper clip.

8. To make stripes, tie a different color yarn to the clip each time.

9. Continue weaving back and forth until you cannot fit another row in.

10. To finish the weaving, knot the end of the weaving yarn to the nearest corner of the warp.

← back

11. Turn the loom over. Cut the first two warp threads in the middle of each thread. Pull them out of the loom's slits at the top and knot them together on the front of the loom, near the weaving. Now pull the same two threads out from the bottom slits and do the same.

12. Cut and tie each pair of warp threads the same way.

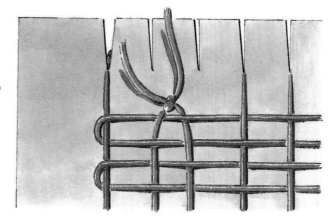

13. After you have knotted each pair, you will find an extra thread at each side at the start and end of the warp. Knot these to the nearest pair now.

The earliest Navajo weavers made blankets that were often worn as clothing and had simple patterns. During the 1800s many weavers began using more complicated designs. Triangles, rectangles, and other geometric shapes were woven in. Some weavings contained pictures of animals, birds, or people. Today, Navajo weavers make rugs, blankets, and other weavings, some of which they sell and some of which they keep. There are many styles of Navajo weaving. Each weaver does things a little differently, making each creation unique.

Secret Code

On a battlefield during World War II, a group of U.S. Marines huddle in a pit while the enemy shoots overhead. One of the marines, a Navajo, has a two-way radio.

"Send a message that we need help," gasps an officer to the marine. "Use code."

Holding the radio to his lips, the marine utters a few words in Navajo. A crackly voice answers on the other end. "They said help is on the way," says the marine.

"Good job," says the officer. "The enemy is always listening to our radio signals, but they'll never break this code. Not one of them speaks Navajo!"

In this code, hundreds of Navajo words were given secret meanings. For example, the Navajo word *lo-tso* usually means whale. In the code, it meant battleship.

Some Navajo words stood for English letters. The Navajo word *ba-goshi*, meaning cow, stood for *C*. *Wol-la-chee*, meaning ant, stood for *A*. The word *a-woh*, meaning tooth, stood for *T*. So one way to say the word cat would be to say *ba-goshi, wol-la-chee, a-woh. (C-A-T)*.

Just to make things more difficult, more than one word could stand for each letter. *Be-la-sana*, or apple, also stood for *A*. So did *tse-nill*, or axe.

Below is a secret message followed by some letters in Navajo code. Use the key to decode the secret message. (See answer on page 47.) Then try writing a message of your own.

A-woh lin ah-nah
gah ne-ahs-jah wol-la-chee be
yeh-hes klesh
klesh wol-la-chee ma-e ah-nah.

Letter	Navajo Word	Meaning of Navajo Word	Letter	Navajo Word	Meaning of Navajo Word
A	wol-la-chee	ant	N	a-chin	nose
B	shush	bear	O	ne-ahs-jah	owl
C	ba-goshi	cow	P	bi-so-dih	pig
D	be	deer	Q	ca-yeilth	quiver
E	ah-nah	eye	R	gah	rabbit
F	ma-e	fox	S	klesh	snake
G	klizzie	goat	T	a-woh	tooth
H	lin	horse	U	shi-da	uncle
I	yeh-hes	itch	V	a-keh-di-glini	victor
J	yil-doi	jerk	W	gloe-ih	weasel
K	ba-ah-ne-di-tinin	key	X	al-na-as-dzoh	cross
L	ah-jad	leg	Y	tsa-as-zih	yucca
M	na-as-tso-si	mouse	Z	besh-do-tliz	zinc

Kneeldown Bread

The year is 1960. You are helping a Navajo grandmother make a kind of food made from corn called kneeldown bread. Outside the hogan, a fire burns in a pit. Inside, you are scraping fresh corn from the cob. The grandmother kneels before a large flat stone, which she uses to grind the corn into a paste. As you work, she teaches you stories and songs about corn. "If you take care of corn, it will take care of you," she says. "Shield it with your body as though it were your own mother or father. Then it will protect you. It will give you good health."

The grandmother shows you how to wrap a little paste in a corn husk, making a packet. Your first packet falls apart. You keep trying until you do it well.

"When the fire dies down, I'll put the packets in the pit," she says. "I'll cover them up with damp leaves and dirt, and build another fire on top. When we dig them out later, they will be ready to eat."

You will need:

- oven
- one ear of corn, with untrimmed husks
- blunt table knife
- plate
- tablespoon
- resealable freezer bag (one-gallon size)
- strong cutting board
- hammer
- baking sheet
- pot holders
- cooling rack

1. Ask an adult for help. Preheat the oven to 400 degrees Fahrenheit.

2. Husk the corn carefully, one leaf at a time. Throw the silk away. Clean and moisten the husks.

3. Use the knife to scrape the corn kernels onto the plate. Throw away the cob.

4. Spoon the kernels into the plastic bag. Let out as much air as you can, then seal the bag.

5. Put the bag on the cutting board, and mash the corn with the hammer.

6. Spoon 1 to 2 tablespoons of corn paste onto a wide husk. Roll the husk into a tube, so the edges almost meet.

7. Wrap another wide piece of husk around it the other way.

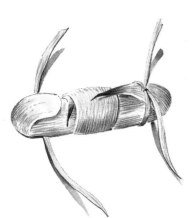

8. Fold up the packet's ends. Tie a strip of thin corn husk around each end of the tube to keep it closed.

9. Put the packet on a baking sheet in the oven for about 40 minutes. The husks will burn, but the inside will not.

10. Take the baking sheet out of the oven with a pot holder. Place the packet on a cooling rack. Let it cool for 10 to 15 minutes.

11. Once it is just cool enough to pick up,  eat your kneeldown bread, scooping out the corn with a spoon.

A Hopi cliff dwelling

4

The Hopi and Zuni

The Hopi of Arizona and the Zuni of New Mexico have been neighbors for centuries. They have often visited each other, sharing customs. Unlike many Pueblo people, the Hopi and Zuni live in the desert.

The Hopi have lived in the same place from the beginning. Their pueblos stand on flat-topped hills called **mesas**. Many Hopi still keep their traditional ways. Even those who live off the reservation return to their family's pueblo for religious holidays. Hopi men farm and weave, while women make baskets and pottery. Their Pueblo ancestors practiced these skills a thousand years ago, using many of the same techniques.

Both the Hopi and Zuni are expert farmers. Their desert land is difficult to grow crops on, so they have had to find ways to grow their beans, squash, and, most importantly, corn. Traditionally, the Hopi have planted their corn deep so its roots can search out water. The Hopi channel rainfall toward their fields with ditches.

Zuni Indian dancers in traditional dress at the Pueblo Cultural Center in Albuquerque, New Mexico.

Many Zuni and Hopi rituals are meant to encourage rainfall. They honor the spirits who bring their crops to life, who bring the rain, and who give the people everything they need.

Hopi Pottery

It is 1930. A Hopi grandmother is shaping moist clay into a bowl. She coils thin clay ropes around the edges of a clay disk. Her skillful hands press the sides firmly.

"I'll smooth the bowl with a piece of **gourd,**" she says. "When it's dry, I'll coat it with watery clay called **slip**. Then I'll polish it with this." She hands you a small smooth stone. "This pebble has been in my family for a long time. It came from a stream near here."

You turn the pebble over. It looks like an ordinary stone, but you know it is much more. You give it back.

"Would you like to make a pot?" the grandmother asks.

You will need:

- 1 or more cups of self-hardening clay, such as Marblex or Das Pronto
- pencil, small sharp rock, or other clay tool
- cup of water
- small smooth stone
- tempera or acrylic paints (yellow, black, white, and red)
- paintbrushes
- stapler
- jar of water

You can put your finished pot somewhere special. Do not use it to hold food or anything wet.

1. Thwack, or throw, the clay hard onto the waxed paper. Knead it a little. Repeat these two steps a few times. Working the clay gets out air bubbles that might cause cracks.

2. Make a clay ball and flatten it into a disk shape, a quarter- to a half-inch thick, for the base.

3. Use a clay tool to make lots of little lines like sun rays around the outer edge of the base. Do not cut all the way through.

4. Roll a thin clay rope, long enough to fit around the base.

5. Coil the clay rope on top of the little lines, following the outside edge of the base. You may need more than one rope to go all the way around. Press it down. Coil another rope on top of the first. Add ropes until the pot is the size and shape you want. Now and then, press the walls together between your hands to keep them even.

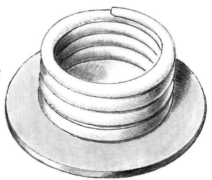

6. Smooth the sides of the pot with damp fingers, inside and out.

7. Let the pot dry. Allow several days.

8. To polish your pot, moisten the outside, then rub it with a small smooth stone.

9. Once your pot is completely dry, think of a design that means something to you or just looks nice. Paint the inside or outside or both.

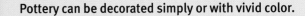
Pottery can be decorated simply or with vivid color.

A Pueblo woman named Nampeyo gave new life to ancient pottery designs. In 1895 her husband began helping to dig up pottery from an ancient Hopi pueblo. The elegant patterns on these pots inspired Nampeyo. She began blending their designs with her own ideas. Other Hopi potters followed her lead. Today, Hopi pottery is admired for its artistry and often seen in museums.

Hopi Toy

It is 1890. You and a Hopi boy are guarding a flock of sheep from coyotes. The boy shows you a toy he is holding.

"It's called a buzz," he says. It's a small clay disk painted with a red, white, and black star and pierced with two holes. A string runs through the holes.

"Watch," he says. He holds an end of the string in each hand and makes circles until the disk whirls. "Now listen." He holds his hands near your ear.

"Bzzzt," says the buzz.

You will need:

- newspaper
- acrylic paints
- fine-tipped brushes
- jar of water
- large button, at least 1 inch across, with two holes
- piece of thin string or embroidery thread, about 3 feet long

1. Spread the newspaper over your work surface.

2. Paint a design on the button, and let it dry.

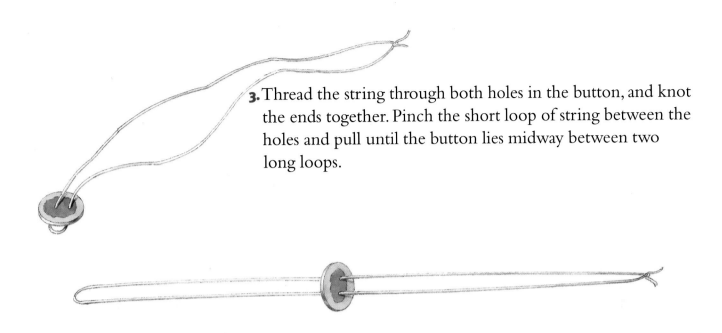

3. Thread the string through both holes in the button, and knot the ends together. Pinch the short loop of string between the holes and pull until the button lies midway between two long loops.

4. To play, hold the buzz in your hands as shown. Make about ten quick circles with your hands, moving them together in the same direction. (Pretend you are jumping rope.) This twists the string on both sides of the button. Then bring your hands toward each other and away from each other, back and forth. Listen for a soft buzz. It may take a little practice, so don't give up!

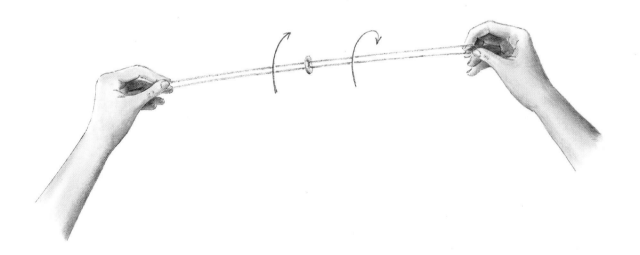

This Zuni boy is wearing traditional jewelry.

Zuni Fetishes and Jewelry

At Zuni pueblo, a jeweler is carving tiny stone animals to string on a cord. You watch, amazed, as a little bear takes shape in his hands.

"Non-Indians call these animals **fetishes**, he tells you. "Zunis have been carving them for hundreds of years. When we make them for ourselves, they are part of our religion. The ones we make to sell aren't sacred."

He shows you a finished necklace. You admire the birds, bears, and other animals. "I learned to carve stone when I was a teenager," he says. "I helped my uncle make necklaces like this. We also made earrings and bracelets from turquoise, silver, and other colored stones."

You will need:

- oven
- aluminum foil, 1 sheet, 1–2 feet long
- Sculpey*, 1 block, about 2 by 2 by ½ inches; you can use different colors for each animal shape if you like
- blunt knife
- toothpick
- skewer, either metal or wood
- ovenproof bowl, at least 2 inches narrower than the skewer is long
- pot holders
- 10 to 20 beads (more, if very small)
- dental floss or beading cord, about 1 yard

*available at craft stores

1. With an adult's help, preheat the oven to the temperature on the Sculpey wrapper.

2. Spread out the foil. On it, slice a piece of Sculpey about a quarter-inch thick. Lay it on its side, and carve the shape of an animal with the knife. (Do not mold it with your hands.)

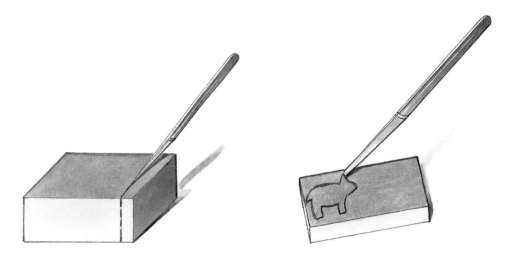

3. Stick a toothpick through the animal's middle. If you are carving a bear, pierce it from the top of its back through to its stomach, and out again. Wiggle the toothpick to enlarge the hole.

4. Make three or more animals. String them on the skewer so they do not touch. Lay the skewer across the top of the bowl. Put the bowl in the oven for about 15 minutes.

5. Take the bowl out with pot holders. Set it on the stove to cool.

6. While the animals cool, tie a big knot a few inches from the end of the floss. Push the other end through a few beads. Then add your cooled animals, with beads in between. Tie a knot after the last bead.

7. Tie the ends of the cord together, and try on your necklace.

Zuni Waffle Garden

It is 1910. A Zuni girl and her mother water their vegetable garden. Corn, tomato, bean, and squash plants stand in squares of earth, surrounded by low dirt walls. Around the garden, a fence of wooden poles helps keep out animals and children.

With a gourd dipper the woman scoops the last water from a clay pot onto a bean plant. "We need more," she tells the girl. The girl balances the pot on her head and hands you another. You try to copy her, but your pot won't stay on your head. Laughing, you both head for the river.

Because of their squares, Zuni gardens look like huge waffles. That's why English-speaking people called them waffle gardens when they saw them. Today, most Zunis buy vegetables instead of growing them.

A waffle garden

You will need:

- walnut-sized lump of clay (any kind)
- newspaper
- 4–6 toothpicks
- green paint
- paintbrush
- 2 cups sand
- 1 cup cornstarch
- old pot you do not need for food
- large spoon you do not need for food
- 1½ cups warm water
- stove
- disposable aluminum pan, about 9 by 13 inches
- paper towels
- square wooden block, 1–2 inches per side (alphabet block or the back of a square rubber stamp)
- green tissue paper
- scissors
- optional: 12 or more small twigs

1. Put the clay on the newspaper, then stick the toothpicks into the clay. Paint the toothpicks green.

2. Have an adult help you make fake dirt. Mix the sand and cornstarch in the pot with a large spoon. Add the water. Cook over medium-high heat for about eight minutes, stirring the whole time, until the mixture gets thick. Set the aluminum pan on a towel or cooling rack. Empty the "dirt" into the aluminum pan. Cover it with damp paper towels.

3. When the dirt has cooled, remove the paper towels and spread the dirt evenly.

4. Press the block into the dirt six to eight times, as shown, making squares with spaces in between. Build up low walls around each square.

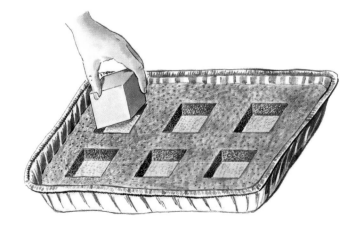

5. In some squares, stick a toothpick cornstalk. Cut thin bits of tissue paper with pointy ends. Stick them on the cornstalks. Fold the ends up, then down, as shown, to make leaves. Place crumpled tissue paper in some squares for other vegetables.

6. If you like, arrange twigs upright around the edges for a fence. Build up the dirt around the base of the twigs.

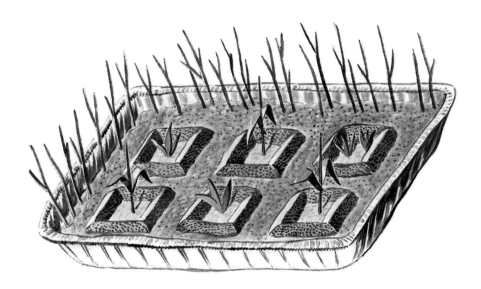

7. The model dirt will harden in about a day.

Glossary

adobe: Clay mixed with straw, used in the Southwest for building.

fetishes: Sacred stone carvings that Zuni people wear or carry.

gourd: A fruit related to pumpkins. When it is dried, its seeds rattle inside.

hogan: Traditional one-room Navajo home of wood and mud.

mesas: Hills with flat tops and very steep sides.

pueblo: Spanish word meaning village, describing the small towns of some Southwestern Native Americans. The people living in these villages are called Pueblo Indians.

reservation: A piece of land set aside by the U.S. government for Native Americans.

sacred: Holy.

slip: Thin, watery clay for coating pottery.

turquoise: Blue-green stone often used in Southwest Indian jewelry.

warp: The threads first strung on a loom.

yucca: A plant with spiky leaves that grows in the Southwest.

Metric Conversion Chart

You can use the chart below to convert from U. S. measurements to the metric system.

Weight
1 ounce = 28 grams
½ pound (8 ounces) = 227 grams
1 pound = .45 kilogram
2.2 pounds = 1 kilogram

Liquid volume
1 teaspoon = 5 milliliters
1 tablespoon = 15 milliliters
1 fluid ounce = 30 milliliters
1 cup = 240 milliliters (.24 liter)
1 pint = 480 milliliters (.48 liter)
1 quart = .95 liter

Length
¼ inch = .6 centimeter
½ inch = 1.25 centimeters
1 inch = 2.5 centimeters

Temperature
100°F = 40°C
110°F = 45°C
350°F = 180°C
375°F = 190°C
400°F = 200°C
425°F = 220°C
450°F = 235°C

Find Out More

Web Sites:

Anasazi Heritage Center
www.co.blm.gov/ahc/hmepge.htm

Hopi Cultural Preservation Office
www.nau.edu/~hcpo-p

Indian Pueblo Cultural Center
www.indianpueblo.org

New Mexico's Pueblos and Reservations—Navajo Nation
www.newmexico.org/culture/res_navajo.html

Books

Bial, Raymond. *The Navajo.* New York: Marshall Cavendish, 1999.

————. *The Pueblo.* New York: Marshall Cavendish, 2000.

Hucko, Bruce. *A Rainbow at Night: The World in Words and Pictures by Navajo Children.* San Francisco: Chronicle Books, 1996.

Keegan, Marcia. *Pueblo Boy: Growing Up in Two Worlds.* NY: Cobblehill Books, 1991.

————. *Pueblo Girls: Growing Up in Two Worlds.* Santa Fe, NM: Clear Light Publishers, 1998.

Noble, David Grant. *101 Questions about Ancient Indians of the Southwest.* Tucson, AZ: Southwest Parks and Monuments Association, 1998.

Roessel, Monty. *Songs from the Loom: A Navajo Girl Learns to Weave.* Minneapolis: Lerner Publications, 1995.

Shemie, Bonnie. *Houses of Adobe.* Montreal: Tundra Books, 1995.

Swentzell, Rina. *Children of Clay: A Family of Pueblo Potters.* Minneapolis, MN: Lerner Publications, 1992.

About the Author

Marian Broida has a special interest in hands-on history for children. Growing up near George Washington's home in Mount Vernon, Virginia, Ms. Broida spent much of her childhood pretending she lived in colonial America. In addition to children's activity books, she writes books for adults on health care topics and occasionally works as a nurse. Ms. Broida lives in Seattle, Washington.

Answer to secret code: The road is safe.

Index

Page numbers in **boldface** are illustrations.